TO WALK
THE NORTH
DIRECTION

TO WALK THE NORTH DIRECTION

poems

C.L. Downing

MoonPath Press

Poetry
ISBN 978-1-936657-82-7

Cover art: North Direction, photograph by C.L. Downing

Author photo: C.L. Downing

Book design: Tonya Namura, using
Adobe Garamond Pro (text) and Josefin Slab (display)

MoonPath Press, an imprint of Concrete Wolf Poetry Series, is dedicated to publishing the finest poets living in the U.S. Pacific Northwest.

MoonPath Press
c/o Concrete Wolf
PO Box 2220
Newport, OR 97365-0163

MoonPathPress@gmail.com
http://MoonPathPress.com

To Veterans for Peace,
the marginalized,
& those who need to borrow hope
until they can locate their own

Show me the steep and thorny path to heaven

—William Shakespeare, *Hamlet*

Contents

TO WALK THE NORTH DIRECTION

The Language of Wind

I am the child of the North Direction:
I am called the Shadow Walker.
To walk the North Direction is to know and hear the voice
of Ancestral guidance, messages light as vapor trails.
Listen, listen, listen for the calling—
The whispers through the trees
calling you home, home, home—
To unchecked cautions and unbridled joys.
I am arias lifting from the small of a back,
sex that pulsates and courses through veins,
dance that is propelled and driven.
I have a maverick's disregard for convention
and shun rumination.
I do not simply 'appreciate' Earth—
I am its direct relative, responsible for its well-being.
I am alive. *A'ho.*

Multiple tribes use the word *a'ho* at the end of a prayer,
similar to the use of "amen."

A Ride in the Rambler

My brother and sister fight over who gets "the good seat;"
the bad one has an L-shaped tear
with a spring that comes up through the spongy stuffing—
my sister says it's like a Leprechaun kicking your butt
all the way to the destination—
she is very wise, my sister.

Mama and Daddy are half arguing—
half playful about punching the radio buttons.
Mama calls the lady who's singing a naughty name
and Daddy defends her saying, "But that's Skeeter Davis!"
in a really important tone of voice.
They settle on Nat King Cole's "Ramblin' Rose;"
my dad winks at us in the rearview mirror because
that's what he wanted all along.

We arrive at Aunt Pearl's and Uncle Vin's just as
the Sears truck pulls away,
to see their new color television set with
a built-in Hi-fi record player.
The grown-ups circle around it like it's a dead 'possum,
staring at the impressive number of buttons and knobs.
My aunt Pearl puts on a 78 of the Mills Brothers
and everybody claps and laughs.

I wake up in the back of the Rambler with "Paper Doll"
swirling in my head and a winter coat over me.
It's dark and the motion of the car leaves me
with one foot in dream-world, marveling about
how my aunt and uncle always
have full candy dishes,
why I didn't get a cool name like "Skeeter,"
and how the quilting in my daddy's coat feels like a lullaby.

Eggshells

All the raging words, the flutter and flight
of discussion, I knew
had to do with me.
She ran her belly (and me) into a dock
while waterskiing, took Dexamyl & prayed,
but I still existed.

"You said I could return to work
When the kids got into school;
I've waited five years…"
Her voice faded.
"Well, now there's another," he said.
A door slammed—
Silence filled the room,
adrenaline filled her body,
a guttural sob of acquiescence
escaped her mouth.

Quietly floating in my amniotic fluid, I sense
she feels trapped,
two prisoners are we.

Barbarism Done Benign

Take away the abusers, remove the neglectors.
There are more effective ways to terrorize.
When I heard Humpty Dumpty had a great fall
I blurted, "Oh no!"
Shushed because there was more & because I made noise,
the narration continued—
They couldn't put him together again…
"That's awful!" I cried out.
The book slammed shut with exasperated
finality, my mother stalked out.
We'd already had disarming discussions
about Georgie Porgie bringing girls to tears,
Jack and Jill cracking open heads,
and the faulty bridges of London that
no material could make safe.

My father suggested stories might work better—
The following night, my mother returned with a big book
of fairy tales—
by the Brother's Grimm.

What sadist thought of the grand idea to put children to sleep
by reading tales of broken bodies unable to be mended,
people poisoning each other,
wolves that devour small children and the elderly?
Benign barbarism—
reigning its own special brand of terror.

Delicate Things

Feathery arms of algae lazily rise and fall
like breath in the salty water of the tide pool.
Creatures dart and scuttle—hermit crabs side-stepping
past purple and orange clusters of sea stars
making a path to shelter
under the slick golden kelp bands.
Sea anemones wait with open mouths
of sea-foam green; a billion molecules of sustenance
drifting.
My tiny brown six-year-old feet are swallowed
by wet sand where I perch, squatted
at the edge of the Divine. Tidal and circadian
rhythms tug and pull at my core and spirit;
I sway and swirl
the way flow tides seep into the pools,
my mind eddying in the gentle churn.
Toppling over in my reverie, other children laugh.
But I care not about their indifferent folly—
they are the children who poke sticks
into the sea anemones forcing retraction and shrinkage,
mustering a false sense of power harming something
so delicate.
I know what it is to shrink back and make yourself
small from Power.
My aunt June told me Mermaids could only be seen
in certain light—those glints on the water are catching
the sheen of their mother-of-pearl scales when
they roll over near the surface. If the whole ocean glitters
there are thousands of them in pods.
So I rise and fall with the feathery arms of algae,
contentedly peering, wildly moved
by the infinity of my micro world,
letting the earth's rhythms pulse
through my bare feet.

Dilution

"Molestation" is much the preferred word—
it softens the blow,
wraps it tidily in less offensive paper
rather than say,
left with a raging wound that resists packing
where the tidal bleed can never be staunched,
or shell husks of a person that maggots
feed off because they live in a state of chronic
decay.
Even "sexual assault" or "rape" should be the go-to.
With "molestation"
you can practically place a bow on top.

Wild World

When a footfall lands near wild strawberries,
exclamations of elation abound,
discovery of a rogue wild rose in the woods
produces *oohs* and *ahhs*…
I dream a world where wild children
would be so loved.
Their feral selves with hardened hearts
annealed with the salve of worth.
But dreams writhe like smoke wisps
evaporating into unseen molecules.
Empty as desire, worthless as hope.
Wild children stay forever in shadow
much like poisonous nightshades
people know not to touch.

Shortcomings of Superheroes

My best friend Jeannie and I scramble with purpose,
lifting couch cushions and patting down pockets
in the piles of laundry room pants;
well-practiced and skilled in our search for coins,
our end-mission is Rutter Road store where
comic books call to us like Homer's Sirens.
Triumphant with bounty, I grab Jeannie's hand,
racing up the four blocks and into the narrow aisles
where Ol' Mrs. Renner watches us like potential thieves.
With thirty cents, we have enough for two, so Jeannie
gets *Blondie* and I get *Metamorpho*. Walter Tompkins
sits outside on the sidewalk edge next to his stingray bike.
The Anderson twins are playing with Aggies further down,
their parents are some religion that doesn't allow them
to read comic books; a wash of guilt and
gratitude run over me.
Walter gets up and swings his leg over the banana seat
with a folded *Captain America* in the back pocket
of his Wranglers.
"Wanna see me pop a wheelie?" he yells to us.
He pumps the pedals hard and yanks back,
elevating both bike and ego—
holding it for about two seconds and Jeannie claps.
The Anderson twins act like they don't care.
Walter comes riding up to us and hits the brakes with gusto
to create a rooster tail of dust and dirt with him in the midst,
like a Phoenix grinning. Jeannie's grinning back.
Walter pulls out *Captain America* and says with authority,
"He switched bodies with Red Skull, but is *still*
able to fight for justice." I kick the toe
of my Keds in the dirt,
wondering if you have to be a boy to be a superhero—
one who can change themselves into anything—
and I ache to be either one; to be able to change.

Mrs. Renner comes out of the store, flapping her hands
and tells us to "Scoot!" With relief, I reach
for Jeannie's hand
but Walter Tompkins yells, "What are ya', queers?"
And Jeannie swats me away like a dirty housefly,
running over to Walter's bike.
I am gut-punched stunned, dropping *Metamorpho*,
and with stinging eyes, watch Walter ride away like a thief.

Velveteen Me

I pleaded and begged with them—
offering my allowance,
my stuffed Beanie and Cecil, and the secret
cats-eye marble
I kept separate from the rest under my bed.
But the magic lights
did not, would not tell me
who my real parents were.

I floated above myself
keeping watch from a distance,
staying numb, detached.
It was like that rabbit in the story—
when no one loved him,
he wasn't real.
So I stayed high above myself
scouting for someone who would know
who my real parents were.

I later learned the magic lights were stars
and they did what I did—
existed all the time
but hid during the daylight to stay safe.

A Banner Year

On Memorial Day, Dad hung it off the front porch,
and it always came out on the 4th of July.
He'd brought it home from his ship
when he returned from WWII.
If it wasn't flying, it was folded in a triangle
in the garage.
In the summer of sixty-nine I recognized it
with foreboding dread, sewn to the butt
of my older brother's blue jeans.
The night the three of them crossed paths—
my brother, the flag and my father—
I peeked through an eke of light
in the crack of my bedroom door,
not daring to draw breath.
The muzzle of the gun right at Dalton's temple,
Dad's arm was steady and straight,
a swelled vein pumping in his forehead
and a tremble seething in his jowl.
The shadows on my brother's cheeks
betrayed the tight clench in his jaw—
He didn't blink,
just stood there tight-faced
and defiant;
until the hammer released
and my father's arm dropped with the unspent gun
dangling.
Dad's eyes welled up;
in a voice I'd never heard, he said to the floor,
"This is not my son."
That Memorial Day we didn't fly a flag
nor speak of its absence.
It was just Memorial Day—
a day of remembrance.

October 12th, 1962

My recollections of the Columbus Day Storm are wooly
and vague since I was only four.
The entire Pacific Northwest held in trance under its spell
like black magic spreading fear
under flickering lights and howling winds.

Neighbors gathered at our house. Mama said that was
because Daddy built our home using the new codes.
In retrospect, I believe our home having a chronically
well-stocked liquor cabinet played a role.

Adults mirrored the fallen live wires outdoors—
voices shrill, nervous laughter bouncing off walls.
My clearest memory is that during the blackout—
the neighbor girls and I got to jump on the beds.
Garbage can lids flew like Frisbees, blindly erratic,
glancing off the corner siding of houses.

At its passing, neighbors dissipated, drifting
to their homes.
My parents resumed the pointedly polite silence
they practiced,
the glaring lights returned, and my brother and sister
argued over whether to watch *Gunsmoke* or
the *Twilight Zone.*
The moratorium on bed jumping resurfaced.
That event cemented my committed love of storms.

Rush Hour

Uncle Fred came back from the war "not right"—
words deemed too awful to speak aloud:
shell shock & battle fatigue were bandied about.
At an eight-way intersection in Portland, Oregon,
uncle Fred caused quite a stir.
He grew flustered over which light was his,
horns began to honk, curses were hurled,
his car took a cautious belch forward,
but ratcheting streams of long passing honks
and light color changes left him paralyzed.
Someone yanked open his door—
not to help him, but to rant at him.
Clutching his head, he pushed past
the interloper and climbed onto the hood.
There he sat and wept.

My dad reminded us of the "Uncle Fred Incident"
every time we drove up Burnside or Sandy.
I was about ten.
It always struck me wrong that the words too awful
to utter applied to Fred and not those around him.

Neglect

I loathe Camellia bushes.
The petals of their blossoms
bruise so easily—
brown marks and scars
all over where they'd been
wounded or hurt.
Maybe it isn't loathing,
rather jealousy.

The Tempest

A storm of secrets rained down on the house I grew up in.
Sturdy white brick with periwinkle lined walkways,
manicured boxwood, and a rose garden
completed the picture.
Grand oaks stood sentry, cloaking prying eyes,
and ancient laurels created canopies of solace to hide in—
I knew all the good spots.
But the storms would rage.
Alcoholism seeped through faulty windowpanes,
neglect dripped down the wallpaper,
Drug use mildewed, leaving poisonous black mold.
My mother furiously patching and damning,
but it kept coming.
Tempestuous winds blew police to our door,
guns to solve arguments;
Child rape and molestation leached through the floorboards
like vines searching for sunlight.
Draft dodging, homemade bombs, mixed marriage
bled through the raised ceilings leaving rust ringed stains…
my mother frantically painting over, sealing off
and reframing it all.
Serving up the palatable version
for your listening pleasure,
redirecting one's gaze to the periwinkle lined walkways—
presentation and decorum are everything.

Summer Loom

I would stretch an August day until
it was thin as unspooled threads—
till the weary sky went wheat gold
and faded into a cradle of crimson,
haling surrender to evening.
Perched in the arms of a grand Hemlock
in the timbers of Neahkahnie Mountain,
I watch the moths and bats perform their
twilight dance flitting past the porch light beam,
hearing the quieting of birdsong,
the rise of a faraway owl hoot,
the distant tease of waves whapping
the shoulder of shoreline, then running away.
Woodsmoke drifts and ribbons
through the stands of alders and fir
mixing with brine laden air,
telling me my father had fired up
the stove to quell the grip of night's chill.
I knew I'd be called in soon.
In those precious last minutes,
I gathered up the sounds and perfumes
the way other children put fireflies in jars.
I laid them under my pillow
so that I could spool them together enough
to weave into dreams.

The Well

I wished for Mike and Carol Brady—
I got Peter Pan and Pol Pot.
I fancied a grandmother like
The Blackfeet's Grandmother Moon—
serene, shining, wise…
Mine blasted buckshot over the heads
of suspicious high schoolers
who came in threatening proximity
to her garden.
So I chucked those wishes down a well,
brailled my way through
a life with simmering desire,
percolated laughter (that sometimes poured over),
drinking in random hits of joy,
tasting the splendor of brine air
and brackish waters,
ever a loving dog by my side.
Sometimes, in the quiet of gloaming,
I hear echoes from the well:
the thoughts that were worth only a penny
splashing into a faraway longing.

Tender Riches

The smells were etched into the walls by seasons
and circumstance:
wood smoke, mildew, my father's cherry tobacco,
and of course, salt air.
The flue to the woodstove was so rusted through,
that you could see flames licking its insides dark orange—
the window glass was wavy, the sand-worn floors
covered by threadbare throw rugs, and the Frigidaire
that needed a gentle kick to close.
There was a stand-up lamp with two globes
of dark golden bubble glass
that we'd pick up and move to whoever needed it most.
I've no memory of a weekend or even a summer there—
rather snippets.
Eye dropper moments that settle all trifles
and exalt tiny joys:
my mother pouring bacon grease into the Folgers tin
after breakfast—
we children fairly flying down the narrow switch-back path
in the thick of the woods under the canopy of firs
that darkened the route until
we birthed ourselves into the stark bright gray sky onto
the beach, sun glinting off the ocean, yelling,
"Ollie-Ollie Oxen Free!"
Turning on the flashlight to see the raccoons eating
the pancakes we left them—
stretching an August day until it was as thin
as a spider's web.
When Louis Armstrong died, his music was played
on the scratchy radio all day;
my dad and I were looking out the windows
when the song "Tenderly" came on.
He put his hand on my shoulder,
pulled the pipe from his mouth and said,

"You're livin' a moment of history, kid."
I felt larger than life.
It was seaweed "tails," driftwood forts, Hermit crabs,
and hologram bubbles,
King of the Mountain and Keds full of sand,
agate hunting and cloud spotting;
gorging on huckleberries so fresh
that the sun's warmth dripped off your chin.

My silver hair flies like sea grass in a breeze,
now being in the winter of my years.
An old Satchmo song caught my ear today
and I heard the lyric,
"The shore was kissed by sea and mist, tenderly..."
A quiet joy ushered to my heart
and an old instinct in me sensed
the fragrance of wood smoke and of course, salt air—
a child's voice eddied in my head,
Ollie-Ollie, Oxen Free!

America the Riveting

The ticket window minders ran the spectrum from bored disinterest to Mr. Toad's Wild Ride enthusiasm. Greyhound bus depots acted as a gateway for a 19-year-old itching to see the world east of Oregon. The terminal departure driveways were an artist's pallet of spray paint color, with Rorschach splotches of black oil stains. The air clotted with mirage-like waves of diesel fumes and once you board, the fetid stench of necrotic foods, other people's sweat, and urinal cakes fully completed the glamor of budget travel. With due respect, that constitutes the worst of it.

Despite riding in the entrails of an elongated metal box that moved with remarkable velocity, the best of it, the glory part split wide open the way lightning tears open a sky, as America flew both past and into the windows: Woody Guthrie's America, Simon and Garfunkel's America, Marion Anderson's America. From the Cascade Range to the Blue Ridge Mountains. The blinding vast white of Utah's Great Salt Flats, the pungent waft of corn husk silk from Indiana's cornfields, the magical canvas unfurling of Arizona's painted desert, the Chicago wind fully wrapping 'round my skin pushing against my body, Maine's salty shores marinated in grey, Manhattan's night world of bustle pushing every button of my nineteen years—America sang my name. She shawled over me while the bus wheels rumbled into nights and across lands.

I discovered that Johnson and Johnson's baby powder took the grease out of your hair. I swam from New Jersey to Pennsylvania at a thin point in a river whose name I've forgotten. I too, was "busted flat in Baton Rouge" and wrote poetry about it on the dirty depot floor there. My dreams expanded, my size contracted in the presence of grandeur—the Great Lakes, Gulf of Mexico, the Atlantic, and the Pacific all made hearty contributions to my resizing. Those bodies of water cradling the names of thousands in their watery graves, and thousands more who escaped to tell tall tales of their wild ride on rough seas. The waters that sprawled the kind of berth that defined horizons, spawned quests, harbored untold griefs, and had ever been the source of siren calls.

What started in a 1978 bus depot where the walls were covered in a miasma of soot and oils overlaying declarations of "Andy loves Lana," an unlikely beauty was born. The desire to see and learn and do more. As Tennyson said, "To strive, to seek, to find, and never to yield."

Memory Balm

The third day riding on a bus constitutes delirium
from sleep loss, blue toilet water stench, and
too many overheated, crowded bodies.
I couldn't sleep sitting up no matter the weight
of fatigue riding my shoulders, taunting me.
Despite the woven lives of my best friend and I,
in my family, touching was punishable by
withering stares and awkward withdrawals.
Pascale said, "For crying out loud, your eyes
look like jumping beans, just lay your head in my lap."
An unthinkable offer I'd normally dismiss,
but the odor of urinal cakes is a powerful motivator.
My grateful weary body sank into a fetal curl,
drowsing, etherized; the rumbling of the bus welcome.
Focused on her book, she absently finger combed my hair.
I had never known a sigh, a plate of food, a hug, or
any collection of kind words to resonate so satiating
as that moment.

In spite of the breath of tides, and span of grace
imposing years since that interaction,
one must assuage the onslaught of dithering politicians,
automated "help" lines, and imposing bloodlines.
It is my practice to walk the woods' edge
and let the wind draw up the salve
of said savored moments—
Those infused with pureness and authentic love.
The healing happens before I ever reach my home door.

Momentary Gods and Pancakes

Maybe it's because I'm not a baker. When I think of batter, I'm reminded of a thing I saw on eBay where a woman swore she plopped her pancake batter randomly in a pan and it formed into a figure of Jesus. There was a photo of the Divine Dropping and it was for sale (not the photo, rather the "actual pancake of Jesus").

I acknowledge seeing things in giant crashing waves, sometimes clouds, and on lesser occasions, in the holographic rainbow bubbles in tide pools. I've never seen Jesus in any of these, nor in batter; but to be fair I have Celiac, so I can't eat gluten. Perhaps this is the reason Jesus is missing from my life.

When the dust rises up behind my bicycle wheels, I just see dust, albeit sometimes in particularly nice swirls. It's hard for me to reconcile those who have experienced split seconds of divinity with the people who screamed obscenities at me when I exited the Gay Men's Chorus one year, throwing gravel and chanting that I was a pervert who would go to hell. Or with the church that absolved my uncle Jack of any blame for the rapes of my cousins and me.

There are times—moments really—when I may have seen Jesus too. In the transitory, mesmerizing rush of wild waters, in the eyes of the marginalized who resist bitterness, in the grandeur of a stand of trees that interact with sky and earth more than I'll ever know. I've never called it that—seeing Jesus that is. But it is surely divine agency allowing me to be witness. So I take a momentary breath and ask how my tolerance might grow.

The Nightmare Exchange

In the hours before dawn
I would hear them screaming.
These were the so-called "boat children"
from Vietnam, Cambodia & Laos.

They told me in hushed tones
and abraded voices of
the terror of the boats when
leaving the only home they'd known.

No one knew how long it would take
to sail to a new home—it seemed
worth the sacrifice to stand for days
in urine and vomit and defecation.

Overloaded, the boats met shore
and told the passengers that
first people off could get land
and home for their families.

More than one hundred dashed
to disembark, but the Captain stopped the rest.
Henchmen waiting in the Malaysian bush
rushed out and took their lives.

The henchmen got a handsome price;
the witnesses paid in dividends.
And the children I counseled
woke up screaming in memory.

Now, decades later, I think of
Tak and Pon and little Ki—
and I sometimes wake up in a cold sweat
in the hours before dawn.

Calando
long slow fade

We race time to beat the Eight-Forty-Five—
Biker Laurie, Tricia the Witch, Gay Jo, KC, and me.
The whistle rolls up off the river's surface
and floats across its own echo.
The five of us scramble over the gravel incline
with grass blades poking through,
climb and reach our respective posts.
The din of the Eight-Forty-Five thunders
under our feet, vibrating our very beings,
coming within a hair's breadth of our bodies
when we pierce the air with
our Friday night ritual
of ear-splitting, throat-chafing screams.
The last car has not even passed
before we have spent our demons
and we share self-congratulatory pats.
We are between worlds, the five of us;
but on Fridays at the track's edge
we heal a thousand years in the forty seconds
of that whistle.
It's fully dark and nearby lights from the coffee house
called The Filling Station beckon to us.
We redirect, still smiling, still feeling the thunder;
I have three quarters in my pocket tonight—
besides a cup of joe, I get to hear
Frank Sinatra's "New York, New York"
on the jukebox.
I trail a step behind my tribe before entering
and listen to the night.
I hear the trestle rumble fade on the water:
the whistle keeps sounding
like a distant dream of Satchmo
hitting a long high note.

Mighty Mary

I'd never known a prostitute before, not as a friend anyway. Mary had bone straight, shoulder length, fine sandy colored hair with highlights of blonde. She wasn't at all what I'd thought. Rarely wore makeup, a freckled, brown-eyed pixie with delicate features…and a goofball.

Mary always had us in stitches. When we all lived together, she did a Mighty Mouse rendition with one hand on her hip, she'd step out one leg, thrusting the opposite arm in the air, turning her head sharply as if to fly singing out, "Here I come to save the day! Mighty Mouse is on the way!" We'd clap and laugh compulsively. Oh, how Mary could make you laugh.

Mary didn't stay living with us. Some souls take longer to find rest than others. I'd see her now and then in one of Springfield's dirty doorways. I'd wave but she always turned away, pretending like she didn't see. And I'd pretend like I didn't notice.

I rushed right to the hospital the night I'd heard she was admitted. Her face bruised purple with stitched up lacerations on the side of her head, her jaw puffy. I didn't want to sound like her world shocked me, so I tried to convey sophistication, asking earnestly, "Was it a john that did this to you, Mar'?"

"No," she said in a groggy voice. "I was sleeping in a Goodwill bin on the soft clothes, when someone threw in a TV set that landed on my head," she winced and tried to chuckle.

My chuckle morphed into a full-on guffaw. "A TV did this?" I'd said, stunned. The absurdity of it made me laugh. We giggled together, me giving her sips of water. Oh, how Mary could make you laugh.

But when I left, walking through the dark Springfield streets, my footsteps scraping on the sidewalk in echoes, I thought about Mary. I stilled with the image of her purple face of bruises and blood. Oh, how Mary could make you cry.

The Living Palette

I am the child of cobalt blue—
hearty and uncontained
arias that course and strain,
pulsate like sex in my blood
and touch my history
with the grace of searing pleasures
to summon all things
that propel dance
and resurrect the dreamer.
       But when the music stops
I am the parent of gray—
of ambiguous truths
tangled in the skirts of shadows…
all things untouchable;
one of whom
is apparently me.
What cruel serpent would have me
live in the barren womb
of a comfortless world
without touch, without color?

Basic Training

Four women in full combat gear
mug for the camera—stare back at me
with innocence and bravado.
We joined for absences—
of opportunity, home, support systems.
We weren't the ones who awakened Ares,
God of War—we didn't even know his name.
The pursuit of service and honor placed us
squarely in the shadow of a cobra's kiss.

We belly crawled under concertina wire,
marinating in soil saturated in Sarin & Agent Orange.
We parched and quenched, water rolling over
our tongues, radiating us with Cobalt 60 & Mustard gas.
We marched, ran, and exercised taking deep breaths
of obscene levels of PCBs.

The EPA shut it down in 2000—
153,640 gallons of nerve agents, herbicides,
and ionized radiation leeched into aquifers
that supplied our water.
The army is not required to notify.

We should have known Ares' name.
But we were true believers.

Burn Baby Burn

"Fire in the belly!" "Be all you can be!" "Get fired up!" Slogans to incite, ignite, excite and encourage living on the edge—the thrill of defying death on the pages of peril. "Fire in the hole!" The acrid tang of sulfur and gun powder odor, the tympanic thrum in my ears. "Drive on!" "Hoorah!" Be honorable—I wanted that. "God! Duty! Country!" Be a part of something greater than yourself; ask what you can do for your country. "Lockdown, lockdown—fires take your position!" Words seared into my adrenaline; brought me leaping from the warm comfort of my bed to covering me with combat gear, bare feet to boots, racing to a foxhole.

Each time my Sgt. copped a quick feel, each time I screamed "Cover me!" the soft and good and kind parts of me fragmented and fell away making me sharper, more linear, more chiseled. Each leer and lip lock, each lock and load inventoried in perpetuity in my brain—tiny registers of offense, stacking up sandbags of resistance, numbness, defenses inside me precariously high—get ready, keep vigilant—always on the alert. Balance, balance—they teeter and threaten to topple unceasingly.

"Ruck up!" (time to move out). "Tits up!" (dead person ahead). "All one big Charlie Foxtrot" (cluster fuck). Sing along with the cadence, "We're gonna rape, kill, pillage and burn!" and the stack gets higher, sleep gets leaner, readiness gets sharper, and the air gets thinner. Tightrope walking on concertina wire. It's all about being one of the boys, only I'm not. It's all about embracing the aggression and dismissing the vile, only I don't and I can't. It's going all in…only I don't belong "in."

Silverfish in shower drains, rats and rodents running rampant in streets where school children play crawling on warheads, where raw sewage seeps into rice fields. It's hookworms in the topsoil, cockroaches in the quarters, abandoned Amerasians, beggars, parasites and prostitutes—too much to keep up with. Jackhammering at my privilege, burrowing into my core, nicking away tiny shards of me. Increasing the pounding percussion in my ears, behind my eyes, throughout my head. Grinding my teeth unconsciously, knowing the expectations roll like an unstoppable boulder: higher, faster, smarter, more than, stronger, better, first place, tight group until yeah, that edge is now a razor; my nerves electric current, my heart in a chronic race with my respiration. The alert sirens and flashing lights of gray matter spinning spastically, working their way into a tornado-like funnel of frantic preparedness. Ever vigilant, ever ready, every day, every second.

"So get fired up Kid—get that fire in the belly!" with a *yuk yuk* solid slap on the back. Aspirations of the American Way. But more of me keeps dying. Splintering off, bleeding out, disfiguring like a Picasso. Bits of me swept up and away like smoke off a moth's wing; dust motes of *shoulds* and *oughts* with nowhere to go. A wail chafes my throat, "God! Help me!" But god is a hologram bubble here; visible one second, then evaporates and is gone. What would there be to help anyway? All that fire leaves—is ash.

Broke

It was a Dickensian kind of world—
a culture pinioned beneath war, survival, and loss.
Poverty was widespread in 1982 Korea,
and in towns outside of Seoul and Pusan
beggars salted every sidewalk and corner—
I gave a quarter here, a dollar there
and heard the adage ad nauseum,
"You can't save them all…"
I didn't dare retort it was me I was trying to save;
I'd leave the country unprosperous, but unbroken.
On a day near the DMZ, my goodwill as exhausted
as my body, my tour almost up,
I glanced at my watch in horror—
late had grave consequences;
missing the last bus back to my village
would leave me splayed open for AWOL—
I dashed around a corner and spotted my bus still waiting,
motor running, people boarding;
that's when she grabbed my leg at the ankle.
I hadn't seen her, sitting cross legged on the ground
in her too large colorful dress, weathered skin,
and iron hair.
Momentum made me hop forward on one leg,
"No Mamasan! Not now," I yelled.
Teetering precariously off balance, I jerked the leg
she had hold of forward to break my fall
but my boot came up under her chin
with an alarming, audible clack.
I reeled around in shock and apology—but her face—
something permanent came undone.
It floated up and away from her like a forsaken prayer.
I stood there mouth hanging open,
the bus honked and revved its engine.
My eyes darted from her to the bus—

I couldn't be AWOL.
I left the old woman sitting there,
bereft, penniless, hungry, without hope.
I boarded the bus in leaps and raced to the back
to see her become smaller as we drove away.
I told myself I had no choice,
That I had no other means back to my base.
I didn't weep.

Chae

It wasn't really a loss, you see,
because he was never mine.
He was just another orphan beggar kid.
We met when he was caught stealing food—
kids steal food for one simple reason.
I brought him to my hooch where we sat
on the stoop by the rice paper doors
sharing Ohm rice with our chopsticks.
I bribed the Mamasan in the village with Spam
and mayo—both hot ticket items—
for her to feed him daily.
Neither of us spoke the other's language
but we both loved Roger Miller's "King of the Road."
Over time, I got him a Frisbee
and we shared time sitting on the stoop.
Or he might burst into the hooch pretending to be
a fierce dragon, roaring, with his hands raised
and forming formidable claws.
On February 26th, 1983 he died of the cold.
His absence, knowing how he died—
left me eviscerated, disemboweled.
Over the years, he's become a phantom limb—
I'd swear I could tousle his hair,
hear his giggle tumble out.
When I hear the first few notes and the fingers snap
from "King of the Road," my lips curve involuntarily,
thinking of the boy who was never mine.

hooch: Small studio apartment

36

Leaving a Mark

My name is carved into a red wooden bar top in South Korea
and I wonder who over the years has read it—
Did they ever muse about who I was?
My footprints dent the soil in many an Oregon forest
falling side by side with elk hooves and bear tracks,
now long since mingled with the duff and humus
of a million pine needles and leaf clumps.
Teeth marks from my bite are notched on
the upper inner arm of a would-be rapist in Texas—
hopefully, they left an impression.
Bits of my heart thrive in tiny pockets of hospitality
and more than a few ex-lovers.
The dent in the pillow that smells of my shampoo,
where my laugh lives suspended in time,
where my spirit has been weightless,
where my rage has echoed,
and my thirst has quenched—
let the marks say
I was here—
I counted.

Eighties' Preyers

A grey veil of ash from Mt. St. Helens floated down, initially appearing to be like some kind of dirty blessing—Ash Wednesday run amok—Ash Wednesday on steroids. The volcano blesses you my son, my daughter—go forth and sin no more. But the seemingly delicate ash was laced with microscopic silicon that scratched glass and lungs equally, birds suffocated and fell with a *fwoop* into the accumulation, not even fit for prey.

The same fate-maestro that allowed a volcanic eruption in the Pacific Northwest destined me to join the army, where I accumulated assaults in alarming increase; not by an enemy, but by bored fellow troops. Defenses up like protective hands to wrest away the baton from the conductor who orchestrated this, but escape was an absolute. Ironically, it was the military who taught me Cover and Concealment. I would not be someone's prey.

When I came home, there was a new enemy advancing; an eruption of a virus called AIDS. I watched friends die like the targets I'd just downed in the military. But my country's leaders were like the military's; their inaction spotlighting who counts. Their silence hung full and still as a guillotine dropped repeatedly. I filled my ink with bullets, but it was no match for their weaponized tongues. They made my loved ones prey.

Now with hair light as thread wisps and twice as silver, I breathe a balsam air incensed with sweet sap and sea salt. A day moon, faint and opaque, hangs in the wild vacillations of a March sky over the ocean. My current world shushes the eruptions of the past, quells the molten streams of betrayals and losses like a balm. I sometimes wonder had I been able to believe in Jesus, would it have been different, but I can't even begin to pray.

Are We Done Yet?

I lost Jesus in a laundromat—
an outdoor one at The Sunny South
Trailer court in Orlando, Florida—
had nothing to do with laundry—
the only similarity being…
how fast things pile up.

I prayed as a little girl not to smell
my flesh frying on the coiled electric burner,
that my caregiver's husband wouldn't
yank off his belt, double it & crack it whiplike
before coming after us—
As a young adult I'd prayed with the holy rollers,
their sweaty palms pressed around my face—
I put Holy Water on my wicked forehead,
I genuflected, bowed, and knelt,
took communion & fucked a choirmaster.
I tried to braille my way to God—
overlooking my caregivers, my childhood,
those collective indifferences
combined with what happened in the army,
what happened in Korea,
what happened with AIDS…
what happened last night when Klansmen
surrounded my trailer…

So I'm washing clothes today,
preparing to leave town.
I sit here allowing my thousand-yard stare
to fall on a window of wet clothes
flopping circles in a dryer
and realize—
I haven't got a prayer.

Looking Back...

In the rearview mirror
it looks quite extraordinary;
the air bathed in crimsons
with a shining amber backdrop
like a low-lit stage
in the Orlando night.
Fire makes my heart race,
a cocktail of fear and awe,
and this one is no exception.
Nearly a quarter mile out
I can still see it dance.
I'll recollect this as the night
when fired up by Ernest and Julio,
I boldly told some Klansman to
"Go to Hell! These women in this photo
are veterans and our only color is green!"—
heady in the mix of self-righteousness
and indestructability.
The fire illuminates the rearview mirror,
casting red reflections on my cheek.
The dark billows tether up
and wrench away my naiveté
with little resistance from me.
I didn't see it coming—
until I smelled the kerosene,
dripping greasy gold streaks
down the side of my trailer,
the way a good wine trails down
a crystal glass when swirled…
And in reflection—
I cannot distinguish
between horror and beauty.

The Red-Haired Man

The red-haired man with scarlet patchwork skin
wore the horrors of his history for all to see.
He'd been trapped under a burning car,
the fire chewing, gnashing, and feasting
on anything protruding or raised, like fingers,
lips, ears, or a nose.
The flames ate back the skin, devouring at will,
like a time-lapse withering & browning
of a dying rose,
leaving a rounded head of holes.
The visible parts of him, a series of
flaps, grafts, and marbled textures,
bright pink, rose, and flesh colored,
of such an extreme nature,
of such an overt display of raw pain,
the well-intended cannot help but look away.
His movements a cadence of effort & limits.
We are seldom privy to personal hells,
the histories that broke us, we keep interred,
packed away neatly into mental trunks of
shame, guilt, agony, and secrecy.
A glint of sad eye revealing a tip now & then.
As though to witness brutal truth might be fatal.
One need only see the wide berth given to
the red-haired man lumbering down the sidewalk.

The Mark That Cain Left

Bureau snapshots displayed defined biceps, taut midsection,
long muscular legs, topped off with a head of
sandy blonde hair, wrapping a killer smile
of impossibly white teeth. Shots of Cain and his partner
Dwight tilling the garden, showing off a plump berry vine,
dressed as Carmen Miranda with a headdress of fruits
and feathers, water skiing.

I'd told him I could provide a massage without hurting him
but as he disrobed, I was thankful he was turned away.
My gasp inaudible; my face wore it.
His body an emaciated framework of skin wrapped
taught around skeleton,
Vertebrae popped like a string of fat pearls,
dehydrated muscle around legs no more than
defined straps around bone.
His skin sallow and scaled from night sweats,
cracked and in many places, split and bled.

When weakness overcame, we'd recline on the bed,
me finger combing his hair—
Dwight had asked me if I'd please make contact while
I cared for him; friends had fallen away,
family checked in from a safe distance.
His short stay in the hospital nearly killed him;
not from the pneumocystis pneumonia but because
the nurses were too afraid to bring in his food.
So we watched *Gone With the Wind* for the insufferable
sixtieth time, as I absently pressed
cold compresses to his head.

One day his father checked in.
I whispered over Cain's choking
that the clock had run out; he *needed* to visit—now.

A silence followed by a cracked voice saying, "No,"
and then dial tone. A Father who forsakes his son is
unworthy of the title.

Two days later, Cain didn't wake up.
Dwight told me the coroner's office had just left with him.
I returned to my car, drove away until I could pull off
at an overlook. In my version,
Cain did not *Go to the land of Nod.*
He received a reception of raucous applause
showing up in Paradise wearing
a headdress of fruit and feathers.

The Lumber Mill

My hands are stiff, fat, and gray from cold—
I can't feel the wood grain sanding the skin off
my fingertips or the icy burning in my back—
it's all gone numb.
When the bell rings, everyone races for
the lunchroom—"You're lucky" they say,
"Most newbies start on graveyard when
the building drops to sub-zero temperatures."
With glee they relate how Big Ed lost a finger
on the saws—Arliss pounds the table
in fits of laughter—"It was so frozen, that
poor sonofabitch didn't even know it come off!"
Old Walt taps his coffee cup—"I've got a new one
for y'all: What do you call a
Chink, colored boy faggot with AIDS?"
They collectively roar over the punchline.
Fever rises up the back of my neck
and flushes my cheeks.
Staring quietly down at my gray hands
I wonder how long it will take working here
to lose all feeling.

The Vigil Keepers

My weary head and worn body
find real estate to lay my being down,
knowing that when the night
begins to ache and sag from
the weight of dreamless hours,
that is when they will come,
gathering round my bedside
like dependable vigil keepers:
my every errant word,
the *should-have-saids*
and recriminations lined along
the bedskirts.
The perils of a society gone mad
dancing upon my bedspread
in a merry mayhem kind of way,
while my haunted past kneels in reverence,
praying into my ear
about undeserved good fortune
and being exposed as a fraud.
Like Pixies, Faeries, and Elves of old,
they sprinkle the night
with toxic reflection
and rubbish rumination.
Eventually, they take their leave
and I am wont to know the why.
Is it because
they've used me up and left me spent?
Or is it of my own volition,
exhausted of their company?
It's of no matter to
the vigil keepers.
They have all the time in the world.

Declaration

homage to Helen Reddy

I am not your antique lace, your deferred demeanor
or your parenthetical add-on.
I am female without need for qualifiers or modifications—
far too many words and too much time
has been wasted as it is.
Too much time feeling like a cat in a paper bag, punching
and clawing my way out of conventions, expectations,
limitations and *shoulds*.
I am the slash of a scar where a breast used to be…
I am a womb that has stretched and birthed…
I am the grief that has brought my knees to hit the ground
in unrelenting anguish and yet found a way to rise again.
I have fixed, I have lasted, I have listened
and worked and healed.
I am fierce and authentic love;
I am the hues and shades of pain and triumph—
I am resilience, celebration and song itself—
rising, growing, soaring!
I do not just seek the sky—I am the sky!
I am god! I am earth!
I am.
And it is more than enough.

Bigs

About halfway between Veneta and Elmira
sits the café with the thirty-foot high plywood Indian
out front with the signage: Bigs Hi-Yoo-Hee-Hee.
It's Pearl Winters bottomless cup of coffee,
it's where pickled eggs in gallon jars are a delicacy,
and Esther McCombe's homemade bells
announce your arrival.
God forbid the loggers forget to take their caulks off
or Pearl will nail 'em in the head
with one of yesterday's biscuits.
Frying bacon, fresh donuts, the smell of work coats
fuse the air over the clanking of silver on plates.
Vesta fills the farmers' coffee cups and declares
she's got this whole "feminism thing" figured out.
Leaning into the counter conspiratorially, she whispers,
"Want to grow dope? Plant a man!"
Everybody gets a good chuckle except Virgil
who laughs hard enough to snort
even though he's heard Vesta tell it twenty times.
Common knowledge is that Virgil's sweet on Vesta
going on five years now.
Folks who speculate on such matters agree that
what with Vesta's unfortunately curious skin problem
maybe she shouldn't play so hard to get.
The red Naugahyde booths harbor the lies
of a thousand fisherman and hunters—
never revealing what they know about
the lust of the town's teens
or the ladies' Wednesday morning coffee klatch.
Pictures of pheasants and bird dogs, a movie still
of John Wayne, and a jukebox
that plays only country music complete the picture.
By dusk tonight,
the pick-ups, log trucks, and animal trailers

will roll out.
Vesta and Pearl will lock up the Hi-Yoo-Hee-Hee
and turn off the lights
halfway between Veneta and Elmira.

First Kiss with a Woman

Her lips chanced on mine the way hands
clasp perfectly together, interlocking.
I swore I'd remain cool if this came about—
but that promise became a ship that sailed
the moment her fingertips worked the nape of my neck
and I Niagara-ed myself into an endless freefall,
my heart a dripping comb of chilled honey
slowly thawing a deep sigh
into a primal part of me.

Invasive Things

In early Autumn,
buried amongst the sea oats
and ground flowers
of the vast ocean dunes
a menace lies in wait,
tiny hooklike foxtails
lodge between the pads
of unsuspecting paws.
Witness to my poor pup limping,
I cajole her into lying down
that I can pluck the offending pain—
instantly, she is better.

In early Autumn,
when light fades
and flowers lose their bloom,
my sweet friend fades with them,
succumbing to the melancholic
surge of menacing memory
re-exposed by muted colors
and early dark.
My heart weeps
to know she's in such pain.
I wish a wish so fiercely:
that I could pluck out the offending pain
and she would be instantly better.

For Annie

And there you were
singing hymns to heroin
while I dined on Disney,
believing in faeries
and happy endings.

But that's the way, isn't it?
Good drawn to bad,
light drawn to dark—
same old train,
different wreckage.

And there I was
living on longing,
making failure a habit
I could shoot up my arm—
looking for beginnings.

Smoking Gun

Patches burned into my skin
leaving crop circles of indentation.
My stomach lurched angrily,
reactive over the nicotine gum.
Chantix pills generated night terrors,
making PTSD seem amateurish.
So I opted for hypnotherapy.

Her voice a metronome
for a long slow fade.
I saw myself a boy of about sixteen
in ancient Rome
running ahead on a parade route,
pushing through throngs of onlookers,
down the dusty course lined with stones,
sandals snapping against my heels,
clearing impediments for
the emperor's route.
Anxious to prove my worth,
hoping against hope
for permanent employment.

It took all those things that did not work
to show me a life lived
as another gender
in a different time
at a place I'd never been.
I marveled as I lit a cigarette.

A Paycheck Away

Just two years before, kids came into school bragging
about throwing hot pennies at bums.
The bums would race to pick them up
and burn their fingers. I was the only one
who didn't laugh.
Now, I recollect that gathering with my bare hands tucked
tightly under my armpits in sub-zero temps,
up to my thinly clothed shins in snow.
I know I must pee on my hands soon
to hem the inevitable surrender to graying—
fearful if the frostbite goes too deep,
I'll lose them.
Icy air slices my lungs as I hop from foot to foot,
singing half remembered Christmas carols in French.
My throat restricted from withholding tears
I resist—give one inch the abyss will own you.
There's a tacky café (Joe's Dogs) ahead
with a matronly waitress named Betty.
Sometimes, she gives me free coffee.
Betty knows I lost my job…she doesn't know
their storage shed is where I'll sleep tonight.
The neon light of the café blinks red on half my face.
Betty gently places her hand on my shoulder
and I cringe when she says,
"A penny for your thoughts."

Gods and Prisoners

Prison life is a cacophony of sound—not like the sounds of comfort, nor like the soar of music or laughter. Nearly all the sound is abrasive, rough, angry—directed at disturbing the silence. That elusive silence drives many of the men into a desperation far more frightening or intimidating than which racist group they have to partake in: Mexican mafia, Brood, Aryans, Indian Pride, Irish Pride, everybody's got pride in their mouth, but no one has it in their spirit. The noise relentlessly jarring, filled with ugly words that are spat rather than spoken; there is no relief, no ability to come up for air. The occasional screams land like a fist-punch and locked doors are used to beat against. God is not found here.

Chow time is a series of calculated moves, done like sharks circling minnows. Chatter upsurges and has the pitch of tension laced thick throughout. It becomes a din just prior to a fight or take-down. A strong-arm will send in someone trying to establish themselves to take another person out; it's called a "torpedo." One can feel one's own heartbeat unconsciously keep time with the rising clamor.

Prison is about living with a scream in your stomach that will never pass your lips. It slithers in and coils around what used to be you. Even for me, who only served as counselor there for five years. Like flood waters climbing stairs, surging a caution that grew into a chronic guardedness. My spirit tamped down and cornered like a starving dog.

I returned to the sea and lifted song up, let guards down. Water cleanses, baptizes, nourishes. My need for the water greater than my need for people; that and the thick of a wooded forest where rain can pour over me—wash me, rebirth me and let me hear the true world; the world of hope and resilience getting resuscitated. It's in nature that I find the heartbeat silence that defies hurdles and resurrects my spirit—quieting the chaotic voices of locked men and absent gods.

Fire Pilgrim

Land melts and crackles hot as the River Styx
in that Fifth Circle of Hell.
The blazes hiccup and dive across the forest floor
while flames scramble up the trees like frantic ivy.
Everywhere the napalm drops, it makes an outline
like police chalk outlines around dead bodies;
unlike the bodies,
the life of wood makes clouds in its passing,
billowing skyward, clotting the air.
Clouds that propel and turn in an upward spiral,
resembling a nervous woman gathering and twisting
yarn into unfathomable patterns.
I've never been this close before:
never felt heated radiance
with this intensity.
It is at once both riveting and harrowing.
I find myself slightly alarmed that I feel a fair amount of
comfort in this level of hell.
Perhaps that is just the hubris in me believing
I can outrun a forest fire—
believing I can outrun napalm being dropped
from a helicopter.
That same hubris—
believing I can outrun almost anything—
prejudices, assaults, memories—
is all that stands between me
and the Pilgrimage through Hell.

Shape Shifter

Fresh rain on the forest floor
wafts up and lingers in the air;
an exotic dance partner
seducing me with petrichor fragrance.
Cacophony of Chickadees,
Nuthatches & Warblers
saturate the air with the lilt of music,
overflowing, tumbling, bubbling...
until my heart runneth over
and I become the shaft of light
boring into the waters,
dissolving from solid form
to dissipate into the floating motes of water debris
turning, turning, turning...
Rushing up from the shape-shifting depths,
breaking the surface, shedding water and skin
at once; gulping air,
raising my sodden wings with a great and powerful stroke,
lifting me with rising spirit—
free from gravity's bonds,
soaring, soaring, soaring,
cool air pushing against and past my feathered breast;
I fly toward the sun,
toward a heaven already known.

Nature's Crucifixion

She retreats in full surrender to the dusk,
dipping her rusted toe beyond the Pacific's
furthest sight line;
her radiant hues reflected on
the underskirts of evening clouds in
chronic predictability:
at once a depiction of both
the mundane and the extraordinary,
death and the inevitable resurrection.
The voice of my heart losing language
every time.
Muted by raw beauty.

Smoke and Mirrors

The truck is returning the inmates to the prison
after they've been fighting
wildland fires for fourteen days.
I watch them disembark in
green pants and bright yellow firefighter shirts,
the pungent odor
of campfire satelliting around them—
their faces and hands
bear the look of chimney sweeps.

Malcolm stands off to the side staring absently,
a turbid froth of processing floating around him.
I approach, gently tapping his shoulder,
"You OK?"
Malcolm keeps his gaze fixed ahead and says
to the horizon,
"Something happened out there."
"Sure wouldn't mind some company in my office."
It is more a plea than suggestion.
He doesn't answer but turns to follow me.
Sitting across my big counselor's desk, he shakes his head
at the floor.
"It's hard to explain, 'less you were there," he utters
while looking up
but past me—struggling for words that come in spurts.
"Our crew boss drove us outta the fire zone this morning.
It's usually pretty loud in the truck…
but we was all dog-tired. Anyways, he yells,
'Hey guys! Look out the left side of the truck.'
So we do and we see 'em, you know? Like eighty or more
of 'em." His voice catches
And he stops. The center of his face reddens and his lips
tightly purse. Clearing his throat,
he continues, "There's little kids, old ladies, husbands, wives,

whole families…and
they got signs. Signs with handmade letters.
When we drive by, they start cheering for us."
He takes a deep breath and tips his head back.
"They hold up the signs while we pass;
All of 'em saying stuff like 'Thank you fire-fighters!'"
Malcolm's eyes are brimful and his voice trembles,
but he smiles and presses on,
"We're all wavin' and shit, pattin' each other's shoulders
and laughin' and all."
A tenuous silence stretches—then, as reverently as
 an anthem he adds,
"It's like we meant somethin', you know?"
And our eyes lock in that truth.

This moment
feels like Grace; something holy and fragile
and of life-altering importance.
This moment, delicate as a transparent insect wing—
neither of us speak so as not to disturb this tenuous worth
floating like a mist that will evaporate at any second.

Death Toll

I have never touched her hair before
but these are the virus years
and everything—
has changed.
I pull the brush through the gray tangles
over my mother's crown,
while she absentmindedly stares ahead
into a world she no longer understands.
Her body is here,
but her mind left
when the virus stole all interaction.
The facility she resided in
ceased all get-togethers
and meals with what she called
her "Dinner table family."
She spiraled from repetition to confusion
to not knowing where she is.
The tenacious 92-year-old who
prized her mind above all else
must now be reminded
that she is not wearing clothes;
I pull through the tangles of gray
and wonder...
Wonder how the experts
find a black and white means to
calculate the number of people Covid-19 has killed.

Five Thousand Arrows

Tribal winds with quicksilver sails
sail howling through the plains
carrying the voices of five thousand
candles snuffed—
discarded like garbage,
disappeared like snow melt.
Shawled with generational abuse,
an easy mark for predatory white men.

But my sisters of the plains & pueblos,
Chinook winds and Black Hills mountains—
you who endured calloused tongues
and careless hands, mirthless laughter,
weaponized words & murderous hearts—
you will not be silenced.
In our remembering, we rise—
we are your voice now,
along with brother wind.
Should they drown us out,
we'll dry off and sing.
Should they bury our spirit,
we'll break the husk and rise through the soil.
Should they kill the woman in us,
ten million more will follow…
speaking truth
for those who've been beaten into submission—
holding hope
for those whose arms are weary—
cradling justice
until integrity can be restored again.
Hearts gentle,
souls fierce,

compassion strong.
We are your arrows
and our flight shall not be denied.

There were more than 5,000 Indigenous women missing in
the US in 2021 alone.

Eleventh Hour

Retirement wrapped its arms around me like an old friend,
sweetly scolding, "Where've you been?"
I smiled sheepishly, but the question took up residence
Where *have* I been?
I wanted to be an artist,
a painter,
a writer.
The social and pragmatic demand for a *real job*
crowded against me, leaving no room
for paints or pens.

Instead, pulling lumber at the mill
until my fingerprints faded into the wood,
tractored as a ranch manager, building fences
to lock in livestock—
I later locked in human beings as a prison counselor.
Real jobs paid the bills and piled up:
cleaned building sites someone else created,
held at gunpoint scooping ice cream,
answered phones, served drinks, and saved drunks.

That young woman with the itchy pen and dry brush
remains entombed.
Hoping retirement can multitask
as resurrection.

Katsi Ah Ya
Umatilla for "grateful thanks"

My eyes fix and scan; they rest, drink and savor…
Life force rises in me like breath drawn from
the belly's depths;
rushes my blood with oxygen,
my heart with exultation.
No semantics can deliver just conveyance;
lofty words fail in the breast of divine agency.
The fierce, unpretentious beauty—
the breath-taking, heart-pounding,
stop-you-in-your-tracks
Beauty…
of bearing witness to where the mountains meet the sea.
Each breath taken from air
swollen with pine sap, cedar boughs, and marine salt.
From what fount did this place pour
and how is it I deserve fortune such as this?
May I be forever humbled, forever in gratitude
for my brother the forest, for my sister the sea,
for this world that makes the mundane magnificent.
May I always recollect this as honor
for as long as I am permitted to bear witness
to this cradle of grace and peace
that showers me with untold
rejoicing.

Book Covers

My service dog licks my face optimistically.
"I'm trying," I say, wriggling my shoulders
in a choreographed measure I've learned
helps wake the paralyzed parts of my body from sleep.
After one hour, I have arms and my torso,
so I yank covers back and toss my listless legs
overboard in hopes of motivating them.

If it works, I walk.
If I doesn't, I crumple like a dashed souffle
and find myself in intimate proximity to the wall,
close enough to inspect the paint strokes.

One level living with wide doors assists
navigation, which slowly improves
as long as it's doled out carefully.
I write down what I need to do, in the order
it must be done in,
because I might run out of steam.
My nightmare scenario is that I would collapse
in a public place—
have to explain with my thick tongue and fogged brain
that I am fading into a neuro-toxic attack.
Speed is my asset as I can feel my functional time
has low water in the well today.

I pull into the parking space designated "wheelchair"
feeling heady with victory that I could leave
mine at home—it's a good day.
As I'm clicking the chirp to lock my doors,
a grating voice calls out,
"You have no right to steal a disabled person's space."

I am stung.
Onlookers stare.
Heat flushes up my neck.
Contained anger sets into my jaw.
I fight the impulse to explain.
I take refuge that at least it's just my body—
my mind and heart are not crippled by
presumption and disdain.
With head high,
I go in to get my groceries.

Shell Shock

Where I live, embattled sea treasures
like sand dollars, shells, and conches
get ravaged and razed,
thrown and tumbled in the mobilized flow
of the charging tides,
their rough edges worn down.
Ultimately, brought to shore laying scattered
across the sands
like the wounded soldiers at Normandy.
A few make it in whole, but most are broken.
And some
hold the sound of having been in the ocean
for the rest of their days.

Seekers

When the sun is extinguished at half past four
as is the habit of December,
gently tucking the night into the horizon,
the skies over the ocean bedecked
in such a true dark,
the stars and planets fairly glow.
An elongated ribbon of light from Grandmother Moon
rides the Pacific's surface—
the sea itself, an otherwise black slate,
save for the crab boat fleets.
Tiny floating temporary cities,
their lights scattered as if the heavens
flicked the back of night
and a cluster of stars fell from their place,
landing on the brackish waters.
My cheeks burn from North Wind's rough caress
pinking them raw while I stare
and think about a god I don't believe in…
Holding a prayer with no words,
longing for a home though not the structure;
rather to possess a sense of belonging.
Standing at my lookout,
the achingly beautiful world & I—
the only sound is waves ever seeking shore.

And I Think to Myself

an homage to Satchmo

From the Blue Ridge Mountains to the Cascade Range,
from Mount Fuji, the Himalayas to the Green Mountains
and White Mountains.
The Atlantic, the Pacific, the Yellow Sea,
and the Gulf of Mexico.
Painted deserts, Great Lakes, salt flats and rain forests.
Manhattan's lights, Indiana's cornfields, Chicago's Loop,
Florida's sun, Oregon's rain, and Korea's rice paddies.
I've lived in two countries, nine states, and forty-one towns.

Maid service, armed service, lumber sawyer, and
clothing clerk;
painter, park ranger, prison counselor; union VP, and deputy.
I've held seventy-one jobs, often several at a time.

Catholics, Charismatics, Holy Rollers, Gospel, Baptists, and
a few others unworthy of mention;
I've joined and quit them all.

Held the boat children in my arms to help heal
the nightmare of their war overseas.
Held children of North Portland in my arms to help heal
the nightmare of their war here.
Held grown men dying of AIDS in my arms, because
at the time,
nobody would touch them.
They all touched me.

Dropped on the sands of Bali Hai by private helicopter,
spent Christmas of '79 in a free soup and bread shelter,
lived in Marilyn Monroe's final home in Brentwood,
California, lived in a halfway house on the rough edges

of Massachusetts.
Joined up to escape homelessness, putting a pacifist
in the Army.
Earned five ribbons, two medals, six Letters of
Commendation,
Outstanding Soldier Award and one near miss
on a court martial.

I've been frostbitten, I've been published,
broken into and broken up with.
Held at gunpoint and lucky enough to be held
in someone's arms.
I've been assaulted and I've been civilly disobedient.
I've been harmed. I've been healed. I honestly couldn't say
which one is etched deeper in my being.

I've lived through—
because that's what people say, isn't it—"through"—
one landslide, one fire, a tidal surge, two hurricanes,
two volcanic eruptions, five flash floods and
multiple monsoons,
veritably stunned and profoundly awed by nature.

This isn't just my life.
This is what makes me alive.

Corona Days

After days turned to weeks and weeks to months,
the noticing began.
How during certain moments of morning
when bars of sun cross my kitchen,
dust catches in the slanted light
until a cloud passes dissolving it from view;
but I know it's still there.
How in my silent trek in the forest
a single alder leaf frees itself—
the aimless flutter aided by gravity
allowing it to rest on the woodland floor
where it will assume a new life in the earth.
How I listen to the memory of your breath rush gently
across the percale sheet—
and think how very tide-like breathing is;
musing whether we are descendants of the ocean.
The motes are still there despite the shadow stealing them,
the leaves still exist, despite not living on the tree.
It's you, who I've not seen in so many years,
that I wonder of your existence.
In these times absent of distraction,
the quiet that used to feel like a mourning shawl,
now more resembles the removal of a heavy cloak
when walking into a life—
where an embrace has waited decades
to be returned.

The Gardener

The lapis light of morning diffused by marine mist
paints a canvas of wooly pastels.
The whistling buoy cries out, searing the white air,
returning to the shore like a cherished echo
climbing up the headland to my cabin
at the wood's edge.
I stop my absentminded weed pulling, mid-tug,
perking my head up like Coyote to sniff the air—
receive the whistle that traveled
all this way
to settle in my garden.
I stuff it in my pocket
atop a falcon's shriek, waves lapping,
and the lazy buzz of a dying bee.
My pocket bulges to overflowing.
I will pluck them as needed
to fertilize my spirit.

Illumination

Dusty trinkets and memorabilia pieces on my bookcase,
somehow invested in a bereft kind of communication.
I pick up my grandmother's candlestick maker—
it is all I have of her.
She jumped out a window when my mother was 19, but
lingered a few days before dying.
No one told my mother until after my grandmother
passed.
This made her a walking pathogen
infecting others with the bitterness etched
into the denial of that goodbye.
These trinkets make life from ghosts—
conjuring grandparents
that never were.
Is it my imagination that gives them a disquieting
apparitional quality?
I want to miniaturize me and climb inside
the candlestick maker
until it becomes language.
Until my grandmother has a voice again.
Maybe she would tell me why.

Kingfishers and Demons

Things you say when you don't know
exactly where to place the blame:
"It's the economy."
I could throw blame at the Sandman or
to the lout who gave him a pink slip.
But sundown drags with it the remembrance demons,
and I skate across the surface of sleep
like a Kingfisher over lake water,
never diving under for that soothing
marine hum and twilight kind of dark.
Churning up white and gray matter to capacity.
Seeping in sirens, broken glass, looking over my shoulder,
the acrid stench of cigarettes and stale wine at shelters,
earmarking abandoned buildings that "might be" safe;
listening, listening...
for sound that might be threat—
despite being in my own home, not being homeless,
better than forty years past.

The demons of being trained to kill and singing about it
as though it were entertainment.
Melodies of rape and burning people alive warp musicality.
And the singer.
Memory dirt kicks up like a rooster tail
of orphans, beggars, prostitutes,
abandoned, desperate, destitute;
but I left them to fend for themselves
then got a better life for me.

Demons of homelessness, demons of dying,
Demons of childhood wars, cold wars and injustice.
Dancing in my white matter
waiting for an opening.
Had I been wealthy, I'd have never known these things.

So maybe it is the economy.
Doesn't matter.
It's twilight and my mind will fill to capacity
and I'll skate across the surface of sleep,
like a Kingfisher.

My Mother's Deathbed

I haltingly approach
her dead body—
my hand breaching the air
hovering over her shoulder
then withdrawing before landing…
I hear the voice of Atticus Finch
walking away from the rabid dog
he'd just shot, saying,
"Don't even think about going near it—
It's just as dangerous dead as alive."

Kintsukuroi

My return to Kincheloe Cove was laden with memories
sweet as overripe fruit.
Rumbling over Sea Foam Road, a sprawl of bay
unfurling on one side.
Sprays of huckleberry, Salal, and Salmonberry
salting the other.
It is a trick of memory to think that the light is softer here,
one can take deeper breaths, the sun is warmer, and the rain
feels baptismal.
In the summertime, clouds of dust powder-up and tan the air
behind every car and bicycle.
The Cove has one paved street and two stop signs,
but no one pays attention to the latter.
Rather they roll slowly through looking for small children,
old dogs, or Mavis Tibbets' grown boy Ronnie, who
day-drinks and sometimes wanders.
Not a town or a township, nor is it a city, rather a tiny hub of
a community of less than 300.
The habitants migrate for many reasons, but collectively
it is to have communion with this world.
As clichés would have it, there are wanna-be artists and
writers and some who actually are.
If there is a car stopped in the street with the motor running
and no driver,
there is considerable likelihood that the driver saw a neighbor
they'd been missing
and got out to have themselves a proper greeting.
Here, the word "sanctuary" came to mean something to me.
Something with a significance
I cannot overestimate, because it didn't just resonate,
it built my broken spirit back in the way that Japanese
dynasties repaired broken crockery,
putting gold veins in between the broken pieces to put it
back together again;

highlighting its resilient history—not masking it.
Kincheloe Cove brought me to home—brought me to rest—
brought me back.

Say "When"

My mom would pour a glass
of milk, instructing us to
say "When"
to let her know it was enough.

If you could take a shower in
just a teeny tiny itsy bit of
Napalm and plutonium
would you be OK with that?

Alright Sniveler. Riddle me this:
How about having trace amounts of
white phosphorus and Agent orange
in your drinking water?
Just trace. Hardly any.

Again with the negative…
I'll bet you're a finicky eater too.

On the base I served at
those things leached into our water supply;
plus uranium, nerve and blister agents.
But the army assures me
"The amounts were minimal."

No one asked me.
No one asked me if *any* amount was OK with me.
I unwittingly marinated,
quenched myself with poisons,
never getting the chance
to say "When."

The Other Side of the Rainbow

for Raina

A continent of words and deeds shadowed by winter's slanted light sprawls wide and long until the tongue is left wordless, wounds are left gaping. The reach of the cast shadow rides like a leaden shawl weighing down shoulders and backs, crippling the spirit. And over the horizon they gallop—the real Four Horsemen of the Apocalypse: shame, guilt, fear, and hurt.

Behind the curtain, seasons change, the light shifting ever so. You don't notice at first the easing slant with its incremental illumination exposing the horsemen that scramble for darkness.

Easy to miss layers of pain sloughing off, oxygen returning to the blood, words beginning to tumble from the brain in the right order. The worldview grafted onto a person by trauma cannot withstand the luminosity.

Like sleight of hand or trick of light, shadows know when they've run up against a heart that has broken the harm cycle. A radiance born from the marrow of bone, spreading outward like tendrils, the dark kept forever at bay—rung in by currents of love and hope, rung in by wild cucumber vines draped over moss-laden limbs, rung in by birdsong in brine-thick air.

Silver-crowned spirits walk among us—we who broke the cycles of violence, cruelty, neglect with our backs, our resilience, our courage, dragging behind us anchors of disdain and pain, cankerous and calloused words that we'll abandon in mud and rock. We will recognize one another, we who came from the shadows of winter light. Uniting in fated kinship, forming allegiances, we will sing unencumbered in our quiet victories, creating stories of celebration, valor, and humility. Our pens will become multilayered feathers; wings with which to soar, watching the ropes of our histories fall to the earth, reaching, flying over the rainbow, as we seek more light—ever more light. It's arriving home. Maybe—for the first time ever.

No Stone Left Unturned

Oh my reckless life—it sings to me off-key
in melodious yarns that weave
the atrocious and the foolish into the palatable and rational,
convincing me every risk taken actually a
calculated turn toward maturity,
not the pin-pulling random explosive
it often appeared to be.
Ah, my reckless life—it wooed me with
flowers, forests and paths not taken;
walking into fires, double-dog daring danger,
cavorting at the door of its lair.
Gambles and hazards seducing me to the edges of chance,
narrowly dodging mayhem and peril,
leaving me hungry for just a taste more
of the forbidden, of the tender,
of the I-didn't-know-any-better.
Oh, my reckless life, the soul of
a Romani Traveler in the days of spring and summer,
now, the spinning wheel of winter spins tales
of misspent youth and unbridled daring
in the warp and weft of the loom—
delicious lovers and dances laced with sin,
a tapestry of my life's rhythms.
The overturned stones beckon me to listen, whispering,
"Well done."

Letter to the Reality Editor

The day threatened to behave like an inexhaustible hymn—perhaps well-meaning but brimming with tedium and likely to stay far past its welcome. Then I read the news.

I do not suffer fools, miscreants, the overly perky, or those who bear the weight of heavy chips on their shoulders, well. The cartography of my optimism has run wildly amuck over the years and head-butted time and again against things like health care going the way of Dialing-for-Dollars, integrity becoming a devalued currency, and pinatas being replaced with the marginalized of the week. Enough is enough.

There was a time when the word "reasonable" carried weight—might've been a worthy goal, but that was before the era when those who took the oath to protect the constitution were not mentally wedded to the National Enquirer and donning tinfoil hats. Many current members of congress have clearly eaten lead paint or are the product of a union with first cousins (listen up MTG). Then you've got your Lindsay Graham types with a sexual orientation known to none, but a social orientation suggesting that any partner of his likely has to be sheared in late spring.

Repugnant and vile policies popping up like boils on one's backside. It's as if this news cycle is a swift current sweeping me headlong into a confluence of snarling curmudgeonly destiny. I may not have a choice but to embrace being a growling old woman writing manifestos on how to improve the nation.

Declaration: First—we medicate all the right-wingers. Next—if it's an organ in your body, clothes on your back or happens in your bedroom with another consenting adult, it cannot be legislated. Laws will change: rape gets the death penalty. Full stop. Sexual assault crimes will require three years of listening to audiotapes of survivors. Bullying in schools will immediately have the bully pulled aside to obtain the therapy he needs, and the victim gets free ice cream with their four closest friends. No regulated militia ever used or needed assault rifles; they're out. Bite my veteran ass if you want to cry about it. If you participate in banning or burning books, the new regime will open your eyelids ala *A Clockwork Orange*, so you aren't so freaking blind. One tax code: fifteen percent of your income unless you make under thirty thou'. No breaks, loopholes, subsections or horseshit. So say I—curmudgeon extraordinaire, queen of the naysayers, caller-out of nonsense, and trumpeter for the marginalized.

See what happens when a day starts out like a hymn? It ends with a sermon on my mountain.

Sea Salt

The spouting horn of sea water shoots up
from a black hole in the basalt
like culling memories from the dark unknowns
of my unconscious—
the onset of the memory Geyser as predictable as
a spouting horn,
and most likely to emerge with the first,
second, or third attempt at sleep.
Once the water has reached its peak, it comes crashing
down, dissipating
into sea foam and ultimately just bubbles with
rainbow holograms
that pop and evaporate; as irretrievable
as memory itself.
Like the God who materializes for an instant,
then vaporizes into
a cloud spread so thin it becomes sky,
the trough in the wake behind a boat,
a lingering scent still dangling after the wearer is gone…
nothing one can truly grab onto.
One day, I will take on the great black landscape of
the basalt rocks
and the spouting horn like an unpredictable Geyser,
will ascend skyward
and come raining, showering, deluging down over me—
washing away the indulgence of
selective recollection.
The sea salt both stinging and healing—
stinging and healing.
No more able to separate one from the other
than say,
hologram memories and evaporating gods.

Buffalo Calf Woman

I dwell amongst the lush weathered trees
wearing decades of wind
on their gnarled branches and bent trunks.
My skin and their bark only a whisper of separation.
From a distance, I watch the ocean in its chameleon
forms, ranging from silvery teal to gunmetal gray
and all variations
of shifting, glinting light in between.
Each delicate step in the nearby dunes disturbs
and nudges the sea grass and sea oats, releasing
a lilt of perfume up like fresh cut hay.
I am intertwined and inseparable from it.
This world that is leavened with shocking beauty
and unrepentant violence of weather,
is my nearest kin.
I stare down the throat of 1,000 cherished days,
reliving any and all with untold joys and secret pleasures.
The sea is my emotional ballast and the counterweight
to a world that sometimes seems filled with madness.
I am the Child of the North Direction—I am called
The Shadow Walker and my place in the world
is the world itself.

The Night Sabbath

My eyelids are heavy with sleep and weighted by midnight when an unknown awakens me. Though deep into night's hours, my bedroom is lighted. I realize I've been remiss and have forgotten to turn off the outside light. I drag myself from slumber and stumble to flip the switch—but it is already down. A startle of wakefulness clicks in and I look out the windows.

The Spruce and Firs are backlit with their majestic stoic forms throwing shadows long and wide as Tennyson's web. Grandmother Moon is full with the Budding Trees Moon and in her cloudless radiance, she shines across the land creating a wholly visible night world. I can smell her perfume. In exchange for my stolen breath, my spirit fills like a baptismal font. There in my pajamas, I stand stunned with the wonder of a child—gazing wide-eyed, marveling, grateful for a world I rarely get to see. One that ticks slow and quiet.

The night dew on the floor of the land shines like glittering stars making it more resemble the heavens. Grounded leaves half-lit, half-shadowed lie motionless and tranquil. Land stretches out like a low-lit stage. Any semantic, any trifle of words escapes me as I do not dare wear the bloom from the awe. In a world otherwise polarized, Mother Earth and Grandmother Moon have consolidated a unity of light-giving—a night Sabbath. I want to hold this memory dear—keep it alive with breath and cradle it in my mind's eye for lesser days.

Water Relations

I could never be a raindrop—
the wretched crowding of all of us
plummeting down together
in rushed journeying,
only to slam into earth
and lay helpless atop the ground,
vulnerable to all
until saturation takes over—
then I'd still be stuck side by side with
thousands of unknowns
for who knows how long, evolving
to mere moisture in the earth's top crust.
That will continue until drought sucks up
the last of my life's will.
But as a human I have to wonder,
if my life is so different
than a raindrop's after all?

The God of Drifters & Writers

Comfort called my name in the headlands above the sea—
it's there that I first felt it; because I felt it rather
than heard it.
The whispery overlap of Eucalyptus and Alder leaves
moved by summer breezes.
A sound I recognized without knowing—
an internal recognition—
the translucent voices of Seraphim singing.
It brought the whole of it to me: God is not an entity
to be defined;
rather an essence ever fluid, moments of minutiae:
a finger indentation in dough slowly remerging to smooth,
the scent of disturbed moss dancing in the air
before dissipating,
a foot impression in wet sand fading with time and tide;
it's reading the Divine, raging against Thomas' dying light,
exulting with Whitman's crew,
walking home in Harper Lee's woods…
I take communion in that copse of trees,
inhaling the brine air of the ocean, exhaling
the cedar boughs;
a simple salvation unfurling.
O Captain! My Captain! I yawp keeping time
with the melodious invisible voices heaven-sent—
those overlapping, whispering leaves.

Magic Potions

I got up in one of those moods—you know the kind—where the world isn't at your fingertips rather settled restlessly on your back; where nothing you try to do works—where you long to hear a kind voice call your name, but the only sound is a black housefly bumping furiously against the windowpane.

My footsteps lumber heavily toward the kitchen with the intent of propping up body and soul with the magic of tea. Having lost weight with illness, my pajamas hang loosely, the hem dragging on the floor—not so much child-like, hewing closer to bag lady.

Staring out the window, my eyes fall on lush green foliage and mosses in the foreground, the tree laden forest beyond surrounded by bushes all conceivable shapes leafing out. A green leaf suddenly moves and becomes a hummingbird. Zipping to his next location he suspends himself in flight: body still, tiny wings faster than vision—once again becoming indistinguishable from the greenery. Is that me? I muse. Solely real and animated when in motion, interacting, only to disappear in my own stillness? I open the window, sensing the perfume of last night's moon, to silently cheer him on.

Fragrances of cold spring dawn switch lazily from the milky juice of dandelion stems to the odor of wet horses. Five cow elk thunder the ground with their majestic beings merging into view. Steam rises from their backs as the muted morning sun breaches the tree line. One stops and braces her legs to shake off the early dew like a pup freshly emerging from a lake, the sunlight catching the spray in a rainbow halo around her. With long deliberate strides, far more graceful than their size should allow, they raid licorice ferns and salmonberry buds, disappearing from view into a deep copse of trees.

A flash of yellow not much bigger than a cotton ball pops out of the emerald salal: the first finch sighting of the year. Crisp air wafts in and I sip my warmth, letting my gaze drift to a blur. In the distance, I can hear the whistling buoy out on the ocean. When the mist accumulates, the boats crossing the bar navigate by sound.

This is the same morning where I emerged from my den in a foul state; there was no peal of trumpets, no empire of epiphanies…more like a ruministic recognition leading me to believe that it was not the tea that was magic that morning—it was the world.

Lasting

My spirit migrates like swallows
returning to some haunted core in me—
ghosts having left an odor of fetid decay
from an unknown source...
The swallows fly away again,
chittering over unshared finds.
My vulva tightens, rallying between
terror and defiance,
valor and surrender.
The thundering rush of waves
in my earshot
a profound reminder—
that even bodies as great as oceans
plummet and crash upon the shores
and manage, still, to go on.

Acknowledgments

The author wishes to thank and acknowledge previous publications:

"Buffalo Woman Speaks" was first published in *North Coast Squid*, 2020.

"Calando" and "The Living Pallet" were published in 1998 in *Imbroglio*.

"Calando," "Looking Back," and "The Lumber Mill" were published in 1998 by the Harvard Press as part of the Academy of American Poets Prize.

"Corona Days" and "Night Sabbath" were both published in *Word & Image 2021*.

"Looking Back" was first published in 1997 in *Text Lures Text*.

Gratitude

If not for Butch Freedman, Lana Hechtman Ayers, writing groups, constructive critiques from Mariah Hencke, Kitt Patten, Flo Frewen, and Karen Keltz, I would have turned to dust, not writing anything for another person's eye. I consider each of the aforementioned more than mentors and supporters, they are genuine friends.

Special thanks to Lana Hechtman Ayers and Caroline Boutard for their generous blurbs, both writers whose work I am awed by.

About the Author

C.L. (Ciel Leontyne) Downing has previous work featured in *Imbroglio, Ribbit, Text Lures Text, Word & Image, North Coast Squid*, and *The Timberline Review*. She has won the Academy of American Poets Prize, Honorable Mention for the Elizabeth Lyons Award, and Runner-up for the MoonPath Press Sally Albiso Award. Her first novel is to be published near the end of 2024.

C.L. Downing is also an accomplished photographer of nature, and from behind the lens, even uncovers beauty in the decaying world at large. Her photographs have won awards, are prized by art lovers, and grace many publications, such as this very collection, as well as the cover of the 2023 edition of the literary journal *North Coast Squid*.

Culling from a life of adventure/misadventure, sometimes privilege, sometimes hardship, always hope, she brings an avenue of authenticity and prospect for optimism in a vial of words painted in the colors of laughter, despair, loneliness, elation, and courage.

Milton Keynes UK
Ingram Content Group UK Ltd.
UKHW040636170124
436182UK00004B/215